RECRUITIN⟍ ⎍ARKET

Successfully run a desk, a ⟍ ⎍nd your business – whatever the climate!

Warren Kemp © 2002

For information write to: Recruitment Matters PO Box 1346 Coventry CV6 3ZF

CONTENTS

SOME GROUND RULES FOR SUCCESS

SOME GROUND RULES FOR SUCCESS

Whether you are a consultant, a manager who runs a desk or an owner/director who may or may not run a desk, **this book applies to you.** I'm not going to try and teach 'granny to suck eggs', yet I'm not going to assume knowledge either. You may already be doing some of what we will talk about. Quite likely you used to do some of it and got out of a good habit! If the content inspires you to really make it happen, then great. If it feels more like a kick up the backside - sorry you needed it.

Everyone in your business who runs a desk must become their own cost centre. Every single person must make an acceptable level of contribution to the business (net profit). There is an old saying that 'sales are vanity – profits are sanity'. Adhere to that principal.

If you are too busy working in your business take some time to work on it. Review the way you run your desk, team, office and/or company with an objective viewpoint. Better still, get someone in to do it with you. I was asked to do that for a client

recently, and with a morning of fact finding and an afternoon of discussing the findings and agreeing a game plan, I left the team better monitored, managed and motivated. I received a phone call the next day thanking me for saving her business and her marriage!   There was very little I saw or suggested that she couldn't have done for herself. As is so often the case though, she lived and breathed her business to the point she had stopped looking in from outside. She was too busy working in her business and didn't take time out occasionally to work on it.

Take personal responsibility for results that you are accountable for and achieve. If you run your own desk then whatever fees and profits you bring in is your responsibility. If you manage a team and /or a whole business then take responsibility for those results too. Don't shift the blame to others. I'm not suggesting you take the world on your shoulders. You can still manage and delegate tasks. Simply ensure everyone signs up to the same thought process.

Yes, the market's tough. What are **you** going to do about it? In a tough market if you haven't previously practised and

honed your recruitment consultancy skills, you won't make much money. If you can quickly take on board the processes and skills that great recruiters use (as outlined in this book) you can start making more money tomorrow. You've already started on the way to enhancing your skills and those results (from whatever level you are at now) by taking action and reading this book. That's genuinely great - for you. You had better get everyone in your business to adopt the same approaches and mentality if you aren't going to start carrying passengers.

During the previous boom period too many consultants worked their desk by picking up loads of vacancies, advertised like crazy then spread enough c.v.'s out for their candidates to get jobs. Some never stopped long enough to build up long term relationships. Instead, they played a numbers game against the clock trying to ensure their c.v.'s were on their client's desk before a competitor's were, and very often with many of the same c.v.'s their competitor had. In boom times if you throw enough darts at a dartboard some will stick. If the dartboard represents vacancies and the darts candidates, even if you only have one dart you can throw it enough times to get a result. (Even quicker throw the board at the dart!)

In a tougher market it's the player who has practised his skills time and time again, who will be able to throw their dart with the certainty that it will go in where they aimed, and where it gets the best result. If you want to get better at darts quickly, there's no point watching someone who plays in the local pub team, someone who scores 180 once in a lifetime. Instead watch a world class player who scores 180 once every game!

Read books, watch videos, listen to tapes on recruitment AND TAKE ACTION. If that action doesn't get the result you want, change it and take further action. When you fly away on holiday, the plane is off course 99% of the time. The captain and his co-pilot know where they are starting from and know where and how they need to land. By assessing constantly their flight path and adapting to weather conditions and unforeseen situations along the way, despite any detours and time issues they almost always land on the planned destination runway. Recruitment companies get into difficulty because they either don't have a clear picture of what success is (where they're going) or they don't adapt early enough (if at all) to changes in the market along the way.

If you are the manager or the owner of a recruitment business

you might have a very clear vision of where the business is going and a pretty good idea of how its going to get there. Does everyone else in the business? Are they signed up mentally to that vision? Do they have the knowledge, skills and behaviour (KSB's) to help you all achieve it? Don't be fooled by a busy fool. Be aware what your staff are doing on a weekly, daily or even hourly basis if needed. That doesn't mean the 'Big Brother is watching you' mentality. It's sharing highs and lows. It's monitoring and motivating. It's ensuring that everyone is working to his or her optimum level and that everyone is playing their part in cracking the market in good times and in bad.

M any
O bvious
T asks
I nvite
V ariable
A ctions
T arget
E nthuse

CLIENTS

CLIENTS

What is a client? A client is a company that has paid you a fee for your services in the last 12 months. If they haven't paid you a fee they are not a client. They might give you vacancies and even interview your candidates but that doesn't make them a client.

Take a look at all the placements you made in this last 12 months and write down the companies who paid you a fee. That's the extent of your client base. Anything else is just **a wish list**.

Today's market is really all about consultative selling. Ask a client or potential client what they want today. Don't simply supply what they wanted last time. Times are now changing daily! Never assume knowledge. To assume makes an ASS out of U and ME.

And remember it's all about them. By that, I mean the only important person in your client relationship is the client. If they ask about your own experience and what your company can offer, make sure you sell the information as a benefit for

them. If you discuss candidate's details with the client explain what your candidate could be doing for them. If you mention their achievements, ask the client what that would mean to his or her company if the candidate could achieve the same results for them.

Get personal. Work as hard as you can to build and strengthen or re-forge client relationships. You worked hard to get a client in the first place. You will need to work even harder to maintain one. Be honest with yourself. Are you doing everything possible to look after all your profitable clients. Have you enough time to dedicate to your most profitable relationships. Eighty percent of your income will come from around just twenty percent of your clients.

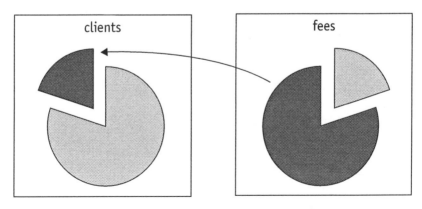

80% of fees comes from just 20% of clients

It would be a good idea if you took some time to analyse where your income has come from in the last year and how many man-hours each client/vacancy took up. The £20,000 deal that takes three months to complete may or may not be more profitable than a £1,500 fee that took less than a fortnight. I was once given four vacancies from a client at salaries of £8,500 and they would only pay me 12.5%. I nearly turned them down as my usual vacancy with them was £20k salary plus at 17.5%. I'm glad I didn't. They actually took on five of my candidates, instead of four, making me over £5000 for less than a third of my working week in man-hours. If I could work those vacancies day in day out that's over £750,000 a year income! Pamper your profitable partnerships.

Keep in touch regularly with your clients whether they have current vacancies or not. When you do, make sure it's for a reason (that will benefit them). In that way they will welcome your contact. I say contact because you should spread the type of contact you make between telephone, email and letter. Vary the reason for your call or email/letter. It might be to present a good candidate, inform them of something happening in their market, or even to ask their advice and make them feel

important. Why not take five minutes right now to brainstorm ideas/reasons to contact a client. Your days will become more varied and you will have more 'tools in your bag' to help build and strengthen your client relationships. A very good gauge of how strong relationships are is how often your phone rings and it's a client at the other end.

Why not consider getting all your clients together for a networking event? I have a recruitment client who used to sponsor tables and awards at industry events. While they always 'paid for themselves' in future fee income, my client felt that there must be a way to get better exposure. We got our heads together and came up with an exclusive dinner. Fifty clients were invited to a dinner in a restaurant hired solely for my client for the night. The dinner was free to their clients and it was 'sold' as a networking opportunity for them to share ideas and information with their industry peers. Each table had one of my client's consultants on it and other than a very simple speech of welcome there was no hard sell. The results were really encouraging with many of the attendees (c.20%) giving the consultants vacancies either that night or within the next three or four days. The majority of them were on a sole agency basis. Most of those attendees would

normally be at an industry dinner where many other recruitment firms would also be there. The cost of sponsoring a table at a typical industry dinner for my client is £10,000. For that you get ten places for dinner and your company name used in various literature and shown briefly on screen a couple of times. The total cost for my clients own networking dinner including drinks and cigars came to £7,000. With average fees for my client being c. £9,500 you can work out the maths yourself with c20% of their clients giving them a vacancy.

How often do you visit your clients? Take the information you acquired from establishing your client list (those that paid you fees in the last year) in one of our previous projects. Review it. When was the last time you visited them? If there are some that you haven't visited in the last six months, that's too long. Your markets changed because their markets changed. Get out to see them. If you don't, a competitor will. Face to face contact wins business. Anything else will help maintain it for a period of time. People buy from people not companies. Keep putting a face to your company's name.

Take time to prepare good relevant questions. Ensure they do

70% of the talking. Listen, really listen, to what they have to say and then act on it. By the way, when was the last time you went on a client visit with a colleague or member of your team? If you are a manager or owner/director it's crucial that you go with everyone at least once in a six-month period. Has everyone had client meeting/presentation skills training either internally, or better still, externally?

Finally there are only three ways to increase your turnover :

1. Increase the size of your client base
   (those paying you a fee)
2. Get clients to pay you more for services you provide
   (bigger fees or higher salary vacancies)
3. Get those clients to pay more often
   (more vacancies or additional services).

… Or, of course, any combination of the above.

LAPSED CLIENTS

In a tough market every avenue open to you to obtain a fee must be considered. That most certainly includes lapsed clients. That's a company who once paid you a fee (but not in the last 12 months).

Lapsed clients who return and become a client again are virtually guaranteed to stay with you – as long as you deliver the results they want. Make a list of lapsed clients and review those company names against your current target list. There will be companies in there that have fallen down the back of the proverbial sofa – literally money lost and forgotten about.

Those that don't appear on your current target list will be those that:

- you or your company failed to deliver for or you let down in some way.
- ones who let you down in some way and/or failed to deliver on their part of a previous bargain.

- you let slip due to lack of vacancies from them.
- your contact changed or moved on.
- or a mixture of the above.

Don't let old negative feelings or disappointments come back to the fore. The fact is they once were a client and you made money from them. It's easier to regain a lapsed client than to find a new one. If they failed to fulfil their side of a previous deal that was most probably one individual in their company. Is he or she still there? Have any restrictive company policies changed?

When market conditions change so do successful individuals way of thinking – and so should yours. Life's far too short to bare grudges. Successful people own up to their mistakes or errors of judgement. Learn from them and move on.

Why not consider what might entice that company to use your services once more:

- an advantageous fee rate
- flexible rebate terms
- being able to head-hunt

Most importantly pick up the phone! Ask them outright.   Tell them that you are sorry you are no longer doing business with them and ask what it would take for them to use your services again. If it's reasonable, profitable and achievable - do it.

I leave this section with a quotation:

"If you have made mistakes...there is always another chance for you...you may have a fresh start any moment you choose, for this thing we call 'failure' is not the falling down, but the staying down."

Mary Pickford (1893-1979)

TARGET COMPANIES (POTENTIAL CLIENTS)

These are the companies who will take up a lot of your time in a tough market. That means whatever it is you do to try to attract them to be a client you had better enjoy it!

If marketing doesn't come naturally to you or its not something you enjoy then take time to work on that part of your business (and not in it). List what aspects of marketing you like and what aspects you don't like. List what aspects you are good at and which ones you are not so good at. Take a look at your 'don't like' and 'not so good at' lists. Use KSB's against each issue to find out what's holding you back from a better success rate. Is it your knowledge, skill, behaviour or a combination?

Only once you have completed that exercise can you really think about improving your success rate. For example - simply making more calls isn't going to increase your fees dramatically if you're not confident about cold calling. Instead, be honest with yourself and ask what's holding you back:

- do you know what to say (knowledge)?
- do you know how to say it (skill)?
- are you nervous about doing it (behaviour)?

Taking time now to complete this exercise and then taking whatever steps are necessary to change things for the better, is time well spent. If it's money invested in training, then that's an investment in future business and profit. If you currently convert say 2 out 100 cold calls into a prospect and you bring in £x of fees per year, what would happen to that fee income if you increased your hit rate to even 3 out of a 100?

So what else can we do with the positive KSB's we do have? Well yes we can make more calls and, in theory, any increase in calls should increase positive results. Why not first, though, review what it is you say when you call up your prospects. Do you:

- say the same things and ask the same questions of everyone?
- have a script?
- use it?
- record the answers formally?
- take action on the facts gathered?

Firstly, I am a firm believer in scripts. A script will do many things for you. It will ensure continuity of message –thus your marketing results are measurable. It will allow you to really develop **how** you say it – not having to try to remember **what** you say. It will allow you to really listen to the answers – we have 2 ears and 1 mouth for good reason!

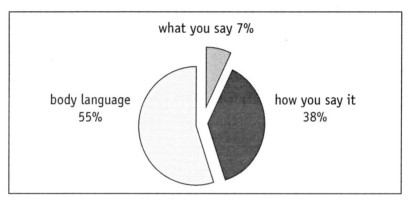

'Effective Communication'

Secondly, recording the answers formally is the only way to market. You can be objective about results when you can review the questions you asked and the answers given. Those results will help build rapport next time you call. Making notes on a dedicated target company form (whether on computer or hard copy) will make your administration easier, keep your desk clutter free and help eradicate mistakes.

Thirdly you should have a number of different reasons for contacting a prospect. The days of the "Hello John, how are you? -I thought I'd touch base again this month. Have you any vacancies you need some help with?" are gone for good (thank goodness). Regular contact will help you convert a prospect into a client and it's simply not good enough to say the same thing every time.

You must call with a reason, and with one that's of interest to your prospect, and one that has some benefit for him or her. Varying the reason for your call will help them enjoy your calls and act more favourably towards you. Each prospect is different and will react positively to different things. That will allow you to have some variation to your day. You will sound fresher and more interested. If one particular type of call isn't working for you that day, there needs to be more in your arsenal. People buy benefits not features, they buy promises you make, and solutions to issues they have.

Why not get one or two of your team together and take 10 minutes or so to think through as many reasons for calling a prospect as you can. Then agree the ten best ones and work on some scripts for them. Here are a few to get you started:

1. Introduce your services
2. Preferred supplier agreements
3. Hot candidate
4. Salary survey
5. Golden question
6. Other services
7. Ask for a meeting

Let's take a look at these options individually:

1. Introduce your services – this is the first call you will make to a potential client. You only get one chance to make a first impression, so prepare well. Make sure you know enough about your prospect's company. If you want to improve your chances for success, read the papers/journals and be up to date. Some simple general rules apply most of the time when prioritising whom to call…. Companies whose share prices are going back up will be more inclined to recruit than those whose are falling. Companies with bigger numbers of staff will be a better bet to cold call than those with smaller

numbers. Remember, its all about them- your 5 years experience is only relevant when sold as a benefit to helping them. Try and grab their attention with a question very early on in your script- they will be forced into thinking about the question, not whether they want to talk to you.

2. Preferred supplier agreements – "Hello John how are you? …Good…the reason for my call today is to discuss how you feel about preferred supplier agreements" is one of the strongest opening lines in recruitment cold calling today –use it. The responses will tell you whether your prospect has one, knows what one is, values them, wants one, or values your calls. You can react accordingly and even the worst case scenario will convince you to stop calling them and to start pulling their staff out instead- that's still a fee to be had!

3. Hot candidate – by far one of the easiest ways to grab someone's attention is to ask them for two minutes to listen to the details you have on a specific candidate who is interested in them and can add value to their company. Make sure you have some really good catchy facts on the candidate and some of their key achievements and entice your prospect into thinking what those achievements would mean for his or her

company if transferred. Stress urgency, and the candidate's keenness to learn more about your target firm. The least you should get in response is "I don't need someone with those skills but you don't have one with the following skills do you?"

4. Salary survey – this one involves a lot of hard work. It will however ensure future business if sold correctly. Ask your contact if they have had an industry specific salary survey carried out for them recently. If there is interest, sell the concept as a confidential survey where all participants (and you will need to sell this to other prospects, too) will receive an up to the minute survey which will help them ensure they are paying their staff appropriately. Stress that this will help them to retain existing staff and ensure future hires accept an offer of employment. Do it free of charge.

5. Golden question – ask every prospect (and existing clients), " What historically is the most difficult position to fill within your department/company?" When they give you the answer, ask another question –" If I came across an exceptional xxxxxx, would you be interested in hearing about them?" No prospect can say no to that question if he or she has his/her own interests and/or their company's interests at

heart. You <u>can</u> ask this of <u>every</u> prospect. If they are less than open with you and you get the feeling they want to end the call before you've had the chance to ask them the golden question, then ask them this question first- " Can I ask you one more question before I go?"

6. Other services – it doesn't matter whether you have other services to offer or not. Ask your prospect whether they utilise, or are interested in utilising, other services to complement their recruitment process. If the answer is 'yes', then discuss the subject matter. If it's something you can provide - then great. If not, find someone who can, split the fee with them and ensure that you facilitate the introduction to your prospect. If you receive enough answers that relate to one specific service and you don't do it, such as psychometric testing, training graduates or reference checking then start doing it!

7. Ask for a meeting – it might not be appropriate to ask this during the first call but it needs to be asked by the 3rd or 4th. People buy from people. Let them see the whites of your eyes. If you're not going out to meet your prospects, someone else is. If someone agrees to meet you, it's not out of politeness –it

is a buying signal. In the last 3 years, I have not been on a potential client visit that hasn't developed into business and a fee. Why? Reasons include determination, flexibility, good presentation skills, confidence and asking for the business, however the one major factor is qualifying them before asking or agreeing to a meeting. That's why the 3rd or 4th call is an ideal time.

Food for thought? Good. So how else can we convert prospects into clients?

Make it as easy as possible for your prospective client to get in touch with you when the time does come for them to use your services. Many consultants phone three or four times, start to build up good rapport, yet have only mentioned the name of their company in the first couple of calls. If a vacancy arises, your prospect must have your contact details to hand. That means emailing or posting those details after the first positive call. By all means give him or her your telephone and email details verbally but don't rely on them filing them efficiently. Make sure you have an auto signature set up for emails too

with your companies full address and contact details as well as your own. Consider an 0800 number as well. Research shows that freephone numbers increase responses to adverts and mailshots by up to 300%

Consider the lifetime value of a prospective client before committing to a certain fee rate. If, say, the average 'life' of a client is 3 years, and that client has c.20 vacancies a year, then you could potentially earn 60 fees from them. If another prospect is likely to only have 3 vacancies per year then that's 9 fees. By taking into account the salary level you will be working at, and the ease of placement, you can decide how much to charge them. My own experience suggests that prospective clients welcome a sliding scale of charges based on your success (starting with your standard terms and moving down after say every 6 placements in a year). Talk to your prospect with the confidence that your budding relationship can develop into a long term mutual partnership – and act like it can and will, too.

Use direct mail. Nothing reaches a mass audience quicker then an efficiently co-ordinated direct mail campaign. An effective campaign should produce a 0.5% to 2% positive

response rate. By following up with a telephone call this can be increased seven fold.   I know you can do the maths, but let's think this one through. All relationships start with a cold call. In order to have one initial conversation, it will probably take you two other calls i.e. To get through to 10 new contacts in a day you will probably make 30 calls (due to your targets not being in, or available, or not wishing to take your call etc). So to get through to 100 people that's 300 calls and that's a big part of any working week!

A well run direct mail campaign can help boost your hit rate, get more people to review your message and give you a foot in the door when trying to get through on the phone, thus cutting down the number of wasted calls. There is an element of luck in any marketing campaign whether it be via post or phone – work the numbers to your advantage.   Here are some basic rules to follow:

• Don't say in your letter that you will follow it up with a telephone call if that's not practical - so work out whether it's a mass mailer or steady drip feed campaign.

• Hand write the envelope and wherever possible send it to a

named prospect and mark it private and confidential - you want your prospective client to open it personally.

- Keep your letter to one page (excluding any enclosures), grabbing their attention from the start – time spent thinking of a good headline or opening is time well spent.

- Send it first class – it's important your recipient believes it's important.

- Send it to arrive Tuesday, Wednesday or Thursday – people generally have more time and/or are better-organised midweek.

- Finally work hard on the content of your letters, having a variety of letters to use, if necessary. If the lifetime value of your average client is, say, even as little as £10,000 - does your first point of contact with them (i.e. your letter) look, feel and sound like £10,000 worth of value for money?

In a tough climate you will have to review (and continually) review how you try to attract new clients far more than in a

buoyant market.   Your job is to make it as easy as possible for your prospect to say yes. Take time with a colleague to list the top ten 'objections' that prospects come up with to your offer of recruitment services. Then work out the best solutions to overcome these - solutions that are practical and profitable.

If for example one of the standard objections is your fee, then instead of reducing it, why not allow the prospective client to stagger the payment over the same period that your rebate terms cover?

What if your prospect has a preferred supplier agreement in place with other recruiters? Then offer to work alongside those recruiters on your prospects <u>most difficult</u> vacancy using your candidates (2 only) as a benchmark?

I'll leave this section with a sure-fire way of picking up new vacancies. It's even possible with this method to create a mini production line of business for yourself. What's more, if you work a vacancy and another recruitment firm makes the placement, it is still possible to get a fee on the back of it anyway! Interested? Good - it's called *'Fill the hole in'*. – and

here's how it works:

Employed people fill the vast majority of vacancies. Simply put that means that in most cases a vacancy arises as a result of someone leaving one employer to work for another. That's where you come in.

Imagine the scenario where you are working a client's vacancy and your are able to put three strong candidates forward and one of them gets the job. You will be one of the first people to know exactly when that successful candidate is going to resign. If your candidate resigns on, let's say, the Monday morning, on either Monday afternoon or Tuesday morning you phone up the departing candidates line manager 'out of the blue' with a hot candidate that you have come across. In the ideal world, of course, it will be one of the two remaining candidates from the vacancy you have just filled or one of the initial batch of applicants i.e. someone who is comparable to the employee who has just resigned.

If you didn't fill the vacancy, you simply ask the client (when he or she tells you that your candidates weren't successful) where the successful candidate came from –and phone that

company up with one of your candidates! When this system is followed religiously almost every vacancy you come across can in itself create another opportunity for you. With excellent timing almost every placement should ensure that you get given the newly created vacancy to work on. How many placements have you made personally or as a business in the last 12 months? What could that fee income have been if you 'filled the hole in' for even 25% of the vacancies created by the assignments you worked on? Don't feel disappointed about it- be excited by the openings that will be created for you this year.

As a final tip, why not keep in touch with companies that advertise their own vacancies- assignments that you <u>don't</u> get to work on. Phone up when you spot an advert and suggest to the named contact that you keep in touch with them so that you are available as back up if their ad fails to deliver. When they make hire without you, you now know the question to ask. Go on –'fill the holes in'!

CANDIDATES

CANDIDATES

'It's not the client who pays you a fee, he only writes the cheque. It's the candidate who pays your fee'.

In buoyant times as we mentioned before, having loads of vacancies to work on and lots of candidates to work with, is a totally different ball game to what we have now. Clearly vacancies are vital – however it's possible with an exceptional candidate to make a placement where a vacancy doesn't exist. It's also possible that by showing a prospective client how good your products are, (your candidates), although he or she doesn't have a need for that particular skill set, he or she may give you a current vacancy to work on.

People in our industry talk about it being a 'client led' market or a 'candidate driven' market – and those two different statements can come from two similar companies in the same market at the same time! Normally what they are saying is that they either have a good number of vacancies or a good number of candidates to work on/with at that particular

moment- or they feel more comfortable dealing with one or the other.

Consistent marketing *will* bring results and the optimum result is that you have a suitable number of vacancies *and* candidates to keep you busy.

If we intended running a desk from scratch today, or our desk had been run down and we were trying to pick it back up again, then would I work on getting vacancies or candidates? My initial concentration would be to uncover 3 or 4 high calibre, placeable candidates. I would then work my market hard, making calls to would-be line managers (not personnel) to discuss their respective attributes, achievements and experience.

So what exactly is a 'high calibre, placeable' candidate?

Well first of all any candidate that you present to a client or prospective client must be good enough to metaphorically 'wave your company flag'. If you have any doubts at all, however small after due diligence, then **do not** put that candidate forward – tough market or not.

Secondly when I say placeable perhaps I should qualify that by adding ' in a cost effective manner'. We have all come across exceptional candidates in our time, I am sure. Very often the exceptional candidate is harder to sell in. They may be for example, paid very well already. They may wish to work for only one of two companies in a large marketplace. They may be harder 'to manage' and so on.

There are no hard and fast rules, simply because everyone is an individual. Try to judge whether to market out a candidate by a quick mental calculation of the number of man-hours you think will be needed to gain a result - versus the fee achievable. Remember, too, that there will be more potential vacancies for middle managers than there will be for senior managers or directors.

Let's look now at what makes a candidate 'high calibre and placeable'. Some simple rules of thumb (and yes there are exceptions to every rule) apply. They must:

1. **Be in employment** – very few potential employers will

wish to pay a fee for someone out of work. That doesn't mean you shouldn't put forward for consideration for a vacancy a candidate who has been made redundant recently. We are talking here however about you actively marketing out a candidate to secure them a move and/or uncover a vacancy. Remember your candidate is your product. Always present your best product first.

2. **Command a salary that is appropriate to their current position/status** – someone who is paid at the very top of the market spectrum will be much, much harder to place. Someone who is paid well below market value will cause concern for a would be employer – "Why is he paid so little and why has he put up with it for so long?" Once again you can present these people when you have a vacancy and are submitting details of 3 or 4 candidates, we are simply talking about taking an individual candidate 'to market' here.

3. **Be realistic about what their next move might be** – that does not mean that they aren't ambitious and confident about their own abilities –far from it. It does mean though that they understand their market value and what steps they may have to take to fulfil their longer-term

ambitions. You want to work with flexible and realistic people.

4. **Have no skeletons in their cupboard** – and it's up to you to ask the right questions to uncover any. We have all probably done something that we wish we hadn't. A good many years ago, I left a well paid job with no job to go to and despite a very good track record up to that point, it took me five months to secure another job. You need to ensure that your prospective client can't say 'no' to your candidate on paper, so that they get the chance to present themselves in person.

5. **Have skills that are needed in the current marketplace** – and current means current! Read well, talk to as many people in your industry on a consistent basis, and be up to date. Present candidates who can add value to a prospective client and who can help keep them one step ahead of their competition (or catch it up). Someone once said – " *If you see a bandwagon, then you're too late*".

6. **Be able to show good solid recent achievements** – nothing sells people better than achievements. Try to keep

the listing and description of the candidates' achievements to the last 18 months and encourage your client or potential client to relate what those achievements would mean for their own company or department. Achievements that particularly sell your candidate will be ones where that person has raised sales, reduced attrition, opened up a new income stream or reduced costs.

7. **Show steady or better career growth to date** – your ideal candidate will have shown steady or better progress with no backward steps. If there are any, sell that as helping his company out in a jam, wanting to see a project through or something else that is positive (if its true). While good career growth is ideal, watch out, however, that you don't frighten a would be employer off – especially if it's your candidates potential line manager who will be doing the interviewing!

8. **Be able to communicate well** – and that's in written, verbal and auditory form. Helping sell your candidate with some ethical enhancing of his or her c.v. is one thing, presenting them as someone better than they are is another. If the role will involve written reporting and

presentation, test your candidates' skills by setting them a project. Many people think that effective communication is about what you say. More important is how you say it. By that I mean the emotions behind the message and the tonality and delivery of it. I've also included in this paragraph the word 'auditory'- god gave us two ears and one mouth to use in that ratio. An earlier diagram highlighted for you that effective communication is made up of 'what you say' –7%, 'how you say it'- 38% and 'body language' as 55%. You must strike the right balance with candidates that you present. Expert presenters will sell themselves to your clients and potential clients when in a meeting scenario – and they will have done that job on you. Don't fall in love with your candidate. Try as much as you can to ensure that they are not 'all mouth and no trousers'. It's easier and safer to help someone enhance their communication skills than to fudge or smudge their career history.

9. **'Look' the part.** – Most of us realise that it is the first few seconds in any interview that will play the major part of a would be employer (and employees) decision as to whether to take the process through to the next stage or not. With

a good positive start the employer will spend the rest of the meeting testing the candidate as to why he or she <u>might be right</u> for the job. With a poor start the employer will unconsciously be justifying to his or herself just why that candidate <u>is not right</u>. The simplest way to help the meeting get off to a good start is for the candidate to look the part – and that means looking as if they will fit in. If they are overdressed or underdressed the result will be the same and it's your job to give them some pointers because you (should) know the company/person they are visiting well enough to help them. Fail to prepare and you prepare to fail!

10. **Relate well to you.** – The candidate does not have to become your best buddy. They do however have to be able to relate to you with respect and value your input. This does not mean that you weed out anyone you don't like - its not the same issue. Simply imagine that your candidate gets a job offer – will they want to discuss that offer with you in depth and really value your help and advice before making a decision? If not, then you are running the risk of not filling the vacancy and disappointing your client. Remember what I said at the start of this section... *'It's not*

the client who pays you a fee, he only writes the cheque. It's the candidate who pays your fee'

OK - so by simply following the above 10 rules we will get ourselves a placement every time- right? If only recruitment and life were so simple.   What the above ground rules *will* do is help you optimise your chances of success. So what else can we do? Well we can take as much time as necessary, every time, to uncover our candidates **'pain and pleasure'** . If it's not something you do now and you start doing it, I guarantee you will make far more placements than you have ever done, NO MATTER THE MARKET CONDITIONS.

When talking with a candidate you need to uncover some form of leverage for use further down the process. This will be vital to sell them an opportunity, prepare a client for meeting him or her, for discussing with the candidate the opportunity after interview/s and to ensure that they say 'yes' and resign. That leverage is their pain and pleasure points. When someone considers leaving a company, or is going to be persuaded to consider leaving, we need them to focus on what they do not enjoy about their current role i.e. what is causing

them pain. We also need to understand what they enjoy about the role i.e. what causes them pleasure. If our client's vacancy is to be a good match for our candidate's needs, (and give us good leverage), then we must offer them an opportunity that matches their pleasure and takes away the pain. Matching the pleasure is essential in 99% of cases – if you take away some of what they currently find enjoyment in, then why should they consider it seriously? However, if you can match the pleasure **and** take away the pain by offering them a solution to the negative side of their current role, you're onto a sure-fire winner (and fee!).

" *When a man talks about his problems he is building a fire. Fan those flames. Because, the higher the flames, the more he will need an extinguisher"*

Pain and pleasure points can be uncovered by asking your candidate what he or she enjoys about their role and noting all the answers (keep asking 'anything else?) and asking them what they would change for the better (again keep asking 'anything else?). Armed with these facts and then highlighting for your candidate all of their pain and pleasure points (pleasure first and pain second) your conversation

might go something like this:

" So John, if I can just quickly run back through the points we have just discussed, so that we are both sure that I understand what you might be looking for in a future move....

If I could put in front of you an opportunity where you could continue to work within a good team environment, where the communication chain was clear and free from company politics and with a company that was in the top ten of their field that would be just as good as you have got right now – is that right? (yes)

However if I were to have an opportunity for you where there are good career opportunities, a far more realistic wage structure, and one that didn't involve so much travel, would you be willing to at least discuss it?"

Once you are armed with these type of facts, not only is it far easier to match a candidate to a vacancy, your chances of it going through are greatly enhanced. At every step of the way you can reinforce just what a difference the vacancy will make to their lives if they get/accept the role. By using this method in c.8 years in recruitment I have only had two people fail to

resign after accepting an offer.

People's pain and pleasure points will fit into the following 5 categories thus making it easy for you use the acronym below as a checklist to ensure you have enough facts to help you sell the opportunity and to aid conversation.

F - finance

A - attitude

C - career

E - environment

D - dedication

- **Finance** – anything at all to do with money, salary, bonuses, car or car allowance, health care, pension etc.

- **Attitude** – the corporate company culture as set by the directors and senior management within the organisation.

- **Career** – how fast, or slow, and what direction their career path is taking, and whether there are advancement opportunities.

- **Environment** – anything that affects your candidate's enjoyment of the daily workplace. These might include colleagues, facilities, where they sit, and how far the journey to work is.

- **Dedication** – how much dedication their immediate superior/s show him or her ie how well they get on with their boss.

None of the above have been placed in any order other than to spell FACED as every individual will be happy or unhappy with different aspects of a job. For example, two colleagues sitting next to each other may view the company culture quite differently, with one revelling in its aggressive marketing policy, while the other feels under pressure because of it. However, what is key is that, well before any offer stage in the recruitment process, you must find out how he or she feels about his or her boss…. (**D**edication).

After all, this is the person to whom your candidate will have to hand their resignation . You simply have to know the

strength of that relationship in order to facilitate the correct end result. If your candidate was hired by their boss as a trainee six years ago, is now a manager and their boss is godmother to his or her 4 year old son, you will have to fan the flames of their pain pretty high to overcome that relationship! It can be done, however. Yet, if you didn't know the strength of that relationship just outlined, how would you rate your chances?

Timing can be everything where the boss —employee relationship is concerned. Catch an employee a week after their boss, to whom they related really well, has left to go elsewhere, and you can really get some leverage. The reason is one of human nature. People are loyal to their boss first and their company second. It's worth stating that again – 'People are loyal to their boss first and their company second'. As soon as you spot someone changing jobs for example in a 'movers and shakers' column in your industry journal you can start to get excited that the named person has left behind some people who are in a fragile state because their 'leader' has left them. Even those who didn't relate well to him or her will be shaky because someone new will have come in, and probably with a proverbial new broom. Get in there and head-hunt

them out!

An even better way to do it is to phone the person who has just moved and ask them for a few referrals of good people they have left behind, people who used to work for him or her. Do you want a script for what to say? OK, try this:

"Good morning is that Tom, Tom Jones?" (Yes)

"Hello Tom my name is Warren, Warren Kemp. You don't know me Tom. I'm an executive search consultant and I work for some of the top names in the industry finding high calibre individuals for them. In basic terms I'm a head-hunter. — *Pause for other acknowledgement*

Firstly, I should point out the reason for my call is not to head-hunt you Tom, I realise you have only recently joined xyz co. Congratulations! You must be really pleased". (Thank you I am).

"The reason for my call this morning is to ask you for some advice if I may?" (Go on) *" I'm working on an assignment for one of my clients who are on the look out for some really good xxxxxxxxx. Is there anyone you might be able to recommend to me, someone that perhaps has maybe even worked for you in the past?"*

Straightforward and effective. What's more by asking Tom questions about why he left, who has taken over from him (if anyone yet), who he replaced at his new company and where

they went to, you can open up numerous opportunities for attracting candidates and by following the chain of events almost certainly find a vacancy too.

Referrals from *existing* candidates are also vital and even more so in the current climate. I'm not a great believer in asking everyone you talk to for a couple of names, as a lot of recruiters are taught to do. It smacks too much of a numbers game and I think people spot that and aren't impressed. Waiting until you have built up a reasonable relationship will get you a better quality of result. Only ask people who you rate highly to recommend friends or ex colleagues. People like people who are like themselves and will associate with that calibre of person – ask an A1 candidate for referrals and you will be given A1 calibre names in return.

Like most aspects of recruitment asking for referrals is all about timing.   So when is the best time to ask a candidate? The day before they go in for their first interview.   Your candidates will be at their most receptive to you in the period between you confirming their first interview date and just before attending it. So when you phone them to confirm their

interview say something like this:

"Great news Mary. As we hoped, xyz co. have just confirmed that they are able to see you on Tuesday at 10.30am. Are you still all right for then ?" (Yes) *"Great. I'll give you a call on Monday afternoon to check everything's ok and cover any last minute questions you might have. Is that ok with you?"* (Yes thanks) *"Good ,now I wonder if you might do me a favour Mary?"* (I'll try) *"Thank you. As you probably know Mary, as a recruiter, high calibre candidates such as you, are vital to me and to my clients. I'm working on an assignment for a client who is on the look out for some good xxxxxxx*. Could you have a think for me and when we talk on Monday could you perhaps give me the name of a couple of good people that you rate highly. I'd really appreciate it".*

- * One of the keys to getting success here is to ask for the names of people whose role is either senior or junior to Mary, i.e. not in any direct competition. By following this method religiously you should be able to replace every candidate in for interview with two more hot prospects thus 'filling your funnel' to ensure steady flow of candidates coming through your system.

The other key time to ask for referrals is, of course, once your successful candidate has resigned. Don't be shy about it either. Ask for as many names as possible and even for their company directory with contact numbers and emails for everyone! Take the successful candidate out for lunch or dinner or celebratory drinks. Work hard on reinforcing the fact that their new role will be taking away their current 'pain points' and how much happier they are going to be in their new job and really get them excited. If you want someone to feel a certain way it will help if you 'go first' and show them how! At the appropriate moment ask for good referrals and then really work your <u>reciprocity</u> card and ask for as much detail as you can and yes even ask for a company listing/directory. One thing is for sure in this life - if you don't ask you don't get.

Reciprocity works, so make the most of it in your business (and personal) life. The law of reciprocity is quite simply that when you do or give something for /to someone they will be happy to do or give you something in return. Smile at someone and you get a smile back. Put your hand out to shake someone by his or hers and he or she will automatically

reciprocate. And so it is with 'favours'. Do something for someone and there will be an unconscious contract formed waiting for them to do something back in return. Just make sure it is all for positive reasons because it also works when you do someone a disservice!

Keep in touch with your candidates and do so for a reason – one that will benefit them or make them feel good. Similar to our client section, take time out with a colleague to brainstorm as many ideas as you can think of for contacting a candidate for a reason. Here's a few to start you off .

Contact them:

1. With a vacancy
2. To refer a friend
3. With a questionnaire
4. With some 'gossip'
5. On a special personal occasion
6. For advice

Lets look a little more in depth-

1. **With a vacancy**- it sounds obvious, I'm sure. Candidates are candidates because they want a change of job. They will want to know that you are considering them for vacancies that you get in *even* if it doesn't quite come off for them. Asking them if they would consider a particular option, even if you think the answer will be 'no', shows you thought of them and gives you an opportunity to run it past them and then ask them if they know someone that might fill the bill. It will occasionally throw up a pleasant surprise. It might well be that you are unsure whether they have got experience of something that your discussions and their c.v. didn't throw up at the time – and they have. It might be that, although they didn't want to consider a certain role 6 months ago, business or personal circumstances have changed very recently and it's now an option.

2. **To refer a friend** – and we are talking here about mailshots or emailshots offering vouchers, a gift or a cheque if they refer a friend to you and that friend is subsequently placed. Make it worth their while and as easy as possible to do. A pre printed form and reply paid envelope for mailshots and a ready-made grid on screen for emailshots will dramatically increase the number of replies. A £150 or even £250 reward is worth them spending five minutes doing it. You might also want to include

a list of some of your current vacancies too.

3. **With a questionnaire** – the list of what the content could be is almost endless. An example might be one that asks them to rate your service to them on a number of points and how your service for them could be improved. You will get some good home truths that you can build on and change accordingly. Asking a question about how they are likely to look for their next job – agency, advert, self, Internet, etc, may then develop into a good marketing piece to sell your services to potential clients. Two birds with one stone!

4. **With some gossip** – not literally of course! We are talking here about snippets of related business news that you have read or that you have heard - snippets that your candidate will be interested in and be grateful for. It doesn't have to be a phone call (sometimes awkward at work). An email or letter, maybe even with a scanned copy or photocopy of an article, is ideal. Remember it's all about regular contact.

5. **On a special occasion** – one that they think " That's really nice". Occasions include birthdays, births (and even deaths), anniversaries, promotions, transfers and when their name

appears in journals. Get to know your candidates and what their values are. Don't become too much of a friend, however, as you want to keep a level of control during the recruitment process.

6. **Ask for advice** – and the advice will probably centre on vacancies and who they know who could be interested. *"Hello John, how are you? Have you got a couple of minutes as I would really value your help and advice on something?"* is the type of approach to take here. If you feel you can do this type of thing with your candidates, then you have been building a good relationship and rapport with them. A good benchmark for your service and future fee income is to ensure that not only can you do this with candidates, but that they are the calibre that you <u>want</u> to do it with.

And, finally, stay focused at all times on the quality of your candidates not the quantity. You are better putting only one exceptional candidate forward to a client than six average ones. Candidates are the only reason you will earn a fee and get return business. A salesperson is only as good as his or her product. Your product is your candidate. Make sure you are spending your time with ones that directly or indirectly will result in

placements.   In your client's eyes you are only as good as your last candidate.

PEOPLE

PEOPLE – YOUR PEOPLE

We are in a service industry, an industry that builds its reputation by the quality of its people and the service we provide. We can't do very much about other recruitment companies, we can only enhance our own company's reputation and hope others are doing the same. A better overall reputation for the recruitment industry is better for us all. That means getting the best out of yourself and your team and constantly striving for excellence. Focus on results, get results.

First, take a good look at yourself and the work you do. Is there someone who understands your business (internally or externally) whom you can sit down with and evaluate your own performance? Someone who you can share your thoughts with and who can help review your strategy for success? Map out an immediate, short, medium and long-term game plan. Agree targets, a time frame and how to go about achieving them. Chunk them down so you know what you have to achieve on a daily basis to achieve the overall target. For

example if you want to gain 10 new clients (companies who pay you a fee) by the end of the year, then work out how many that means per month. In order to obtain that figure, how many calls and visits will you have to make in total and how many will that mean on a monthly, weekly and daily basis.

Targets and goals have to be S.M.A.R.T-
- *Specific, Measurable, Achievable, Realistic & Timely.*

Be as thorough as you can when evaluating your targets and goals. Start by talking about a specific figure or result and discuss how you will go about achieving it. Consider all the options you have available to you to achieve the desired result. It might be that with help from a colleague or by going on a training course you can achieve something. If you engage help where and when needed to enhance your own current knowledge, skills and behaviour (KSB's) you can and will achieve some dramatic results.

Do the same exercise for your company as a whole, involving every relevant person at the appropriate moment. Gain commitment from everyone. Ensure everyone feels part of the process and not simply given a non-negotiable target or

number of targets to achieve. Empower people, not overpower. Take as much time as needed. That does not mean meetings for meetings sake, or asking someone to think about something for two weeks. The appropriate time spent up front will, however, increase your chances of success later. Fail to prepare and you prepare to fail. Your overall company targets and goals may be built up by individuals own targets and goals or those individuals own may be derived from the company's targets and goals. That will be governed by many issues, not least company culture.

The market has changed and that will mean you and your company changing too. It's never easy, yet the worst thing you can do is to stick with the tried and tested where it no longer works. Learn to constantly evolve. Do so with a process in place ensuring everyone benefits from something new or enhanced - that works. Evolving doesn't mean constantly reinventing the wheel. I use with my clients something I called **I.V.O.**

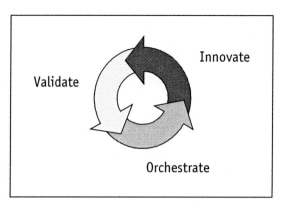

'Perpetual Improvement'

Innovate - come up with an idea, a plan, a system, or a better way of doing something. Discuss and agree the next step

Validate - test it out and enhance or amend your actions, the plan, or the system accordingly, until you are happy with the result.

Orchestrate - roll it out throughout the company ensuring that it becomes 'the way we do that around here'.

Let's then discuss the two main categories of people in your business – the fee earners (consultants and managers) and non-fee earners (administrators and researchers).

Firstly, let's look at fee earners. The ability to prioritise well is never more needed than in a tough market. Too easily, people

can start out their day with a 'to do' list that looks organised and by the end of the day the 'to do's' haven't been done and the days results are less than acceptable. Sometimes the hope of a placement, however remote, makes an individual stop working in a consistent manner. So what should your fee earners concentrate on? Let's prioritise things by asking the question: "What should they work on that will give them, consistently, optimum fee income at maximum net profitability?"

The answer in priority order looks something like this:
1. Retained client vacancies
2. Client vacancies
3. Other current (fillable) vacancies
4. Client relationships
5. Marketable candidates

So, other than helping them prioritise, what else can be done to help your fee earners fee earn to their full potential, other than remembering to take time to talk with them, ask questions, listen and act accordingly? Well, in a buoyant market you can have a team with the right mix of 'finders, minders and grinders'. Maybe it's now time to ensure that

each fee earner is not dependent on someone else to do his or her job. If account managers have less accounts to manage, what are they doing for the rest of their day?

As one of my recent adverts said "Q. What if I invest in training my staff and they then leave? A. What if you don't and they stay?" - If a fee earner's KSB's are not a match for their job description, then do something about it- with internal and/or external training. I know I would rather spend £2000 on training someone who could then earn another £50,000 for the business this year and every year to come, than £2,000 for an advert that may make the business a one off £10,000 in fees.

One such area to enhance their skill could be teaching them how to head-hunt (often called 'search').

15 Quick Tips about Successful Head-Hunting

1. Remember Head-Hunting finds the best available candidates – not the most visible.

2. People like people who are like themselves – learn to mirror and match.

3. It's not what you say but how you say it.

4. The person asking the questions is in control – the one answering is on the back foot.

5. Ask questions of everyone, and read well – people want to talk to people who are in "the know".

6. The best time to get a referral from a candidate is the day before they go in for their first interview.

7. You won't get the business from a potential client unless you ask for it.

8. You only get one chance to make a first impression – prepare well.

9. Uncover candidates' achievements – that's what a client will appreciate.

10. There won't be an issue with fees later on down the line if you bring them up at the start.

11. If a candidate isn't good enough to 'wave your company flag' then don't present them to a client.

12. Tell the truth –nobody ever lost a client for being truthful.

13. If in doubt, leave them out –don't put any old candidate in to make up the numbers.

14. The work you do today affects your business a month down the line – today's placement is last month's hard work - so be consistent.

15. Find a niche area within your market – then become an expert in it.

Your fee earners need to be able to sell a solution to a client that is right for that client. In some cases head-hunting is the answer. If they can't offer that service, they may lose a vacancy or worse still, not deliver on an assignment. Fee earners need to be aware when to offer one of the three solutions available to a client: database, advertised selection or search.

	Specific past experience necessary	Location is a problem	Specific current experience necessary	Confidential	Time critical
Few candidates exist	Advert	Advert	Search	Search	Search
Many candidates but few are active	Advert	Advert & partial search	Search	Search	Search
Many candidates but terms are poor	Advert	Advert & partial search	Search	Search	Search
Many candidates and terms are good	Database / advert	Database / advert	Database / advert	Search	Search/ database

Clearly motivation plays a large part in enhancing fee earners results. Apart from training and good management what else can you offer them to encourage peak performance? Bonuses/commission are part and parcel for the vast majority of recruiters. Are your/their bonus arrangements in keeping with the current climate and does that bonus system encourage or discourage your fee earners to go the extra mile? Are they solely team based? – <u>Think again</u>, split fees for sharing candidates, clients and workload are helpful but in this market you must allow the better recruiters to really shine. Make no mistake - if you change the shape of your business and adopt many of the ideas contained in this book there maybe some 'casualties'. If that is the case, however unfortunate, make sure it isn't your top fee earners. Top fee earners, who can't achieve as much bonus as they are capable of because of others actions/results, will leave you.

Every individual must become an individual profit centre. Calculate each fee earners overall costs as a percentage of their fee income and take appropriate action. Take into account their salary, bonuses, national insurance, advertising spend, expenses and apportion a part of other business overheads on a per head basis.

Make sure every fee earner cross sells other services/divisions within the business every time they make a call. If you feel it worthwhile, reward them accordingly every time they have a hand in bringing new business into another part of your company. The thought that "It's part of their job to do so" works only in theory. The vast majority of recruiters are motivated positively by money. Take 5 minutes to do this exercise now: Work out how many new clients you gained last year as a percentage of your total number of clients (the total number who paid you at least one fee). Now multiply your total overheads for that same period by the percentage figure you just worked out. Divide that figure (still with me?) by the actual number of new clients. That figure comes close to showing you how much it cost you to get one new client. How much would you now pay (as a far cheaper alternative) a fee earner for attracting a new client to your business by cross selling his colleagues services? Put another way, how much emphasis should you now be putting on that area of your business?

Each individual has an individual set of KSB's to bring to your business. Try your best to highlight the most effective and least effective parts of that makeup for everyone. Then review

the seating arrangements within the/each office. 'Buddy up' wherever possible fee earners who can learn from each other or move people around regularly to learn from lots of their colleagues. It only takes a fee earner to pick up one tip that results in a fee when put into practice for it to be worthwhile. Again, increasing your fees and profit in a tough market.

Why not consider staggering the hours people work? Increasing the number of hours people work or enforcing a 12-hour day really isn't very productive. Having people available out of hours for candidates and clients is beneficial, however. Fresh, alert fee earners will achieve more in any environment. I bet you have at least one top fee earner in your business who seems to work less hours than others, yet you also have a 60-hour a week person who struggles to achieve anywhere near their targets. Focus on helping people to get better results from what they do, not how long they do it for. That does, of course, still require people to work the minimum sensible hours asked of them.

Let's now briefly look at your non-fee earners. How many administrative staff do you have? If your fees are down on

this time last year, do you still have the same amount of admin people? When was the last time you reviewed their daily workload? If you feel there is 'spare capacity' at the moment within your admin team (however large or small), firstly make the decision whether to reduce the number. Could you hire another fee earner for the same money or could you just benefit from saving the money? Next, sit down with each of them and really dig in to find out what other skills they can bring to the business. Has one of them got some sales ability and, if so, experiment with them phoning lapsed clients, potential clients, or old candidates. Has another got a methodical inquisitive mind that could do some sort of research role for you? How up to date is your database? Could one of them help cleanse that information?

If you have a research person/team, what has that role entailed in previous months/years and how is it changing or how could it change now? If you are lucky enough to have retained assignments, then the researcher duties will most certainly be focussed on those. Today's climate means there are less retained assignments around, so what are they doing that's productive? My suggestion would be for them to concentrate on the same priority list as covered earlier for fee earners.

It's now part and parcel of a researcher's role to utilise the Internet to uncover information. You need to ensure that all your researchers (or fee earners if you don't have any) can properly source information on-line. Do they understand Boolean logic (commands that generate search results)? Do they know the difference between an anchor, a domain and a link? With c.10 million unique CV's posted within job boards on the www and a further 100-115 million passive candidates details residing elsewhere on-line you have no other option if you are going to succeed in today's recruitment market.

Constantly review all your people. Remember- focus on results, you get results!

OPERATIONS

FEES

OK, so times are tougher with fewer vacancies and fewer good candidates. Some companies will now be hiring without the help of a recruiter because there are now more applicants out of work and going direct. Others will be struggling to attract the right ones with or without a recruiter's help. Your job is to work with your existing clients and attract new ones by putting the best available candidates forward in as timely a fashion as possible, offering excellent value for money.

What do you charge now? Let me word it differently. What do you try to charge and what do you actually charge? If your standard fee is say 20% according to your terms of business, add up all your placement values in the last 12 months and divide the total by your fee income in the same period. Work out the average fee invoiced as a percentage. Shocked? Disappointed? Surprised? Have you or your team too often negotiated fees downwards unnecessarily, or are your standard fees too high anyway?

Like all the questions I am asking you, I do so to prompt thought and then for you to take action where applicable. That action may mean a very simple enhancement or a larger project to uncover the optimum solution. Note down your ideas on the left hand page : notes + follow up + action = change.

First then, review your fees. In a recession should you reduce fees? Will that help or simply reduce turnover and profits? Once you reduce them on an ongoing basis for a client, it's nigh on impossible to increase them for that same client later. Should you increase them now across the board and offer a Rolls-Royce service?

You have to be able to justify your fee – **first to yourself**, then to your clients.

- If you think your fees are too expensive for the work you do –you're right!
- Either upgrade your service or reduce your fees.
- You can't sell what you don't believe in.
- If your fees are too cheap for the service you provide then, downgrade your service or up your price.

Companies don't have money to burn, yet throwing a small or large amount of money at something that doesn't work out is the same result –a waste of money. Clients will be more than happy to pay your fee, whatever the figure, if it represents excellent value for money *and* resolves their recruitment issue.

When was the last time you checked out your competitors' fees? Every 6 months is the minimum you should wait to review them. Don't just find out your competitors' fee rates, try to gauge the level of service provided, too. Ask your clients or potential clients for this information. They will soon tell you what *they* think!

ADVERTISING

Don't!!

OK, so that might be rather drastic. What are your alternatives? Before you start making any decisions, step back a bit and ask yourself these questions? Do you know how much money you have spent in the last 12 months on advertising (both off line and on line)? Do you know where? Do you know when? Have you an accurate costing for each publication or job site? Do you know where and when your best responses came from? Which style, size or type of ads pulled the most responses and which pulled the least? Which style, size or type of ads made you the most placements (quite different from the most responses)?

If you don't have an accurate breakdown of your last 12 months advertising expenditure and profitability, then can you work it out retrospectively? When you have those figures and facts we have just gone through worked out, only then you can start to assess what steps you should now be taking in this tougher market. While that exercise is being conducted, put a

ban on all *non client-paid* advertising. It might seem a big step to ban all ads. It won't be for long, it will save you money and it will certainly inspire those around you to help you get the relevant information.

Once you have your facts and figures, really start to analyse the last 12 months ads closely with profitability being the one constant. If a job-site gives you 50 jobs for a month for £500 and a half page ad (in which you can show 12 jobs) in your leading industry journal costs £500 for one insert, you can only make a judgement on which is best <u>with the relevant facts</u>. If you want a real eye opener take a look at the wording of the current jobs that your staff or colleagues have put on a c.£10 per job pro rata job-site. My research into these shows a lot less care and attention to detail by consultants on cheaper advertising alternatives than on dearer ones.

Another way to review advertising spend is by individual consultants gross fee income and gross advertising spend. Broadly speaking, (and there will be exceptions to every rule), the consultant with the highest percentage of ad spend in your company to overall income (in comparison to your most profitable consultant) is likely to:

- write poorer ads
- place them in publications that yield a poorer response
- not monitor his or her ads as well (if at all)
- not be as commercially astute
- have fewer other recruitment techniques to utilise
- build fewer long term contacts

Your overall advertising spend may represent for example 10% of your fee income. You can, however, dramatically reduce that spend by being fully aware of previous and ongoing results. It maybe that you don't wish to cut ad spend at all, just get better results from it. Constant monitoring is the way forward.

Client-paid advertising is another area where you can enhance your profitability. If you sell client-paid ads at a profit just now i.e. you book the journal space at £x and you sell it to your client at £x & 20%, is there room for an increase in these figures? With a concerted effort can you sell more ads and/or sell them at a higher mark up. If you don't sell them at all can you start? – At least one of your competitors does!

Another option is to reduce your mark up and sell them at

break even or even slight loss. In this way you may sell more of them (or start) thus picking up more assignments and with more client-paid ads and greater exposure there may be less need to place your own generic ads. Think profit at all times.

Just as you may be feeling the pinch at the moment, so are the advertising agencies. There are some excellent deals around if you ask. If you normally use an advertising agency to type set/create your ads and book the space, try to renegotiate the fees they charge you. They will have lost a few clients recently (who have folded or stopped advertising) and they can ill afford to lose another. Ask for a reduction in their art work costs or their set up charges or an increase in the share of the rebate that the journals and publications give them. Most ad agencies will receive between 10% and 15% of the cost of the ad (your ad spent with your money) back from that publication. They will also be on an annual rebate for total spend by all their clients. Get a slice of rebates or start looking for an agency that will. I will happily recommend an ad agency to you who give 50% of their rebate back to their clients and on generic ads, do not charge a penny for production or art work, and they are also one of the major names in the industry. They also charge nothing for work done on client-paid ads

unless the concept is 'sold' and the ad booked.

What about the journals, publications and job-sites? They too are feeling the pinch. If you have a contract with any of them, again try to renegotiate it. If you are an intermittent advertiser with a certain publication, try negotiating a really good deal for committing to a number of column inches with them in a year. This may become a good idea after your review of overall advertising spend, as mentioned earlier. Alternatively, if you have an advert that is not time sensitive i.e. if it can go in either week of two, then have your ad ready and leave it until an hour or two before that publications dead line and ask for a special rate. They will almost without exception be phoning around their regular advertisers to try to sell last minute space (e.g. if they have sold three quarters of a full page). Better still, let them know that you might be interested in last minute space on a regular basis.

Test your advertising. This may seem a simple statement and an obvious one, yet, at some time or other, most of us have fallen into the trap of not testing like for like. The secret of optimising advertising response is wherever possible to only change one element at a time when conducting a test. By that,

I mean if you place an advert in one industry journal in black and white and the very same advert in another journal with spot colour, its not a like for like test. Did the advert with the best response succeed because of the journal or because of the colour used?

Finally, wherever possible, mention in the headline of your advert the three best ways to optimise your response (when used together):

- Job title
- Location
- Salary indication

    ...go on – test it !

VARIABLE AND FIXED COSTS

Whether times are getting tougher or not, the only thing that keeps you in business is net (bottom line) profitability i.e. how much money is left in the bank after you have paid all your bills.

When I'm invited in by a company to help develop their business, one of the first questions I like to ask is how much profit is that company making and what is that figure in relation to gross fee income (turnover). I'm still shocked after over five years of asking that question, how many owners/managers/directors can't tell me relatively easily and quickly (even in percentage terms if they don't want to divulge figures at that stage). Tough times or not, evaluate every decision you make by its profit potential.

Cut out all unnecessary expenditure (for everyone and lead from the front). Check every expense claim and question something in every single one. Its amazing how those claims start to go down in value once word gets around that you are

scrutinising them! Check dates against a calendar for those taxi, lunch and petrol receipts. Is it possible that someone's Sunday lunch with his or her partners till receipt 'fell' in with his or her client and candidate entertainment ones? Does your least productive consultant really travel that many miles on business? Is it possible that by leaving 20 minutes earlier for an appointment your team could take public transport across town instead of a taxi? It's not about being mean or penny pinching- it's about safeguarding people's jobs for the future. If someone in your business has been made redundant recently or there's that prospect in the air now - is it right that people should be even slightly 'carefree' with the company's profits?

Give someone the project of reviewing some of your standard costs e.g. stationery, equipment rental, electricity bills. Then get them to phone up these service providers and ask for a reduction. That's right - ask for a reduction. If, say, your printer is unwilling to review their charges, then get three quotes from alternative suppliers and either ask again armed with these figures or change supplier. I have clients who in recent times have managed to obtain the following:

✔ 10% off their franking machine rental for 12 months – by threatening to terminate the contract.

✔ 30% reduction in printing costs with a current provider – by ordering future supplies less often and in larger quantities

✔ 50% off printing costs –by changing supplier.

✔ 20% telephone call rate reduction- by utilising a discount call provider.

✔ 10% off stationery costs – by changing from a national to a local company (its no longer same day but saves £500 a year minimum).

✔ 12.5% reduction in electricity charges – by changing supplier

✔ 30% off telephone call rates – by questioning tariffs (and they got a £5,500 rebate !) - give me a call and ask me how.

✔ 33.3% rent reduction on their offices for 3 months – by talking about having to reduce their serviced office space (£3500 saving).

My own 0800 freephone number (0800 074 9289 since you ask!) costs me just £2.00 per month service charge compared with BT's £50 a month.   The call charges (you pay for incoming calls with 0800 numbers) are 50% of BT's costs too. If you want to know who my supplier is give me a call.

Sit down for 10 minutes or so with your management accounts or profit and loss and list all the areas with potential for saving money. It might be the most profitable 10 minutes spend this week!

YOUR DATABASE

- How happy are you with your database?
- How many contact companies are on there and how up to date is that information?
- How many candidates are on there and again, how accurate is that information?
- Can you do a search either on the system or manually to show how many of your contact companies have NOT been spoken to in the last 12months?
- Is it possible to do the same for candidates?

If you find out the answer to the last two questions you should immediately be prompted into some form of action.

I have a client who was struggling to make placements, yet had c.4500 candidates on their database. We ran a project where we first searched for how many candidates hadn't been spoken to in the last 12 months. The answer came back at 3000 plus. A little further investigation showed that they had a healthy advertising budget and in order to fill vacancies they were

quite simply working the candidates that came in from adverts alongside some others who were still fresh from other recent ads.   The result was that the database was full of good candidates who were not being searched properly   against vacancies.   It was a very expensive pile of redundant information.

The next stage was to contact every one of the 3000 plus old candidates by letter. With a reply paid envelope enclosed (we set up an account with The Royal Mail for their business reply service) we asked them a few simple questions e.g. did they wish to remain registered, would they like a call, did they have an up to date c.v. to send. My client achieved a 15% response in some form or other, many of which were highly placeable. If, after two months from date of posting, an individual had not responded they were marked as 'dead' on the system. This continued after the first hit, on a monthly basis, thus ensuring that everyone on the system had received some form of contact in the last 12 months. The result was the placing of candidates who would otherwise have been overlooked, more accurate market information and the consultants starting to really network with their pool of candidates.

I should mention that, as an 'incentive' for them to see the project through, and to really start working the database, we took away the budget for generic adverts for three months! Not only did they make more fees (and profit for the business) from the database; they saved a lot of money in advertising overheads as well.

If you feel the need to conduct that type of exercise, I bet you've felt that need for sometime. It takes a lot of input and time and telling your colleagues or staff that the database will be trimmed dramatically, might not go down too well at first. The results will be worth it and in the long term save huge amounts of time on searches. If you put this book down and go and do a search for a current vacancy, I bet you either get huge numbers of unsuitable candidates coming up in the result or barely any at all. Both results would be enhanced with an accurate database with fresh up to date information.

Once you've completed the candidate cleansing exercise take a close look at the client information too. Another wealth of missed opportunities and revenue?

I'll finish this section with a tip. Extract from your database a

list of all the candidates you have put forward for jobs whom you never placed and with whom you are not still in contact over the last 12 months. List the companies you put them forward to and phone them up asking for those candidates by name. i.e.. If you put Joe Bloggs forward to xyz co. and abc co. say 6 months ago, Joe didn't get either job, and since then you have not called him with other opportunities, or when you have, he has said "I'm sorted now thank you" – then give xyz co. and abc.co a call asking to speak to Joe. There are lots of fees to be recouped by doing this exercise. A client of mine has recently started this. They weren't that convinced by my idea and so only really tackled it in a few odd spare moments and yet within the first 50 calls they uncovered 'lost fees' of c. £10,000!

FOOTNOTE

That's it. I hope you have found this book useful and most of all, if it has fired you up to re-evaluate your own way of working and that of your company then it has done its job. Your future billings are in your own hands - no one else's.

It has been my pleasure to have worked with over 300 recruitment companies in a management consultancy or training capacity in recent years. It's the combined experience of the most successful people within those 300 plus companies added to my own, which ensures for you that the content of this book, and the ideas and information in it, are all tried and tested and will make you money - whatever the climate.

Decide the outcome and result you want – agree a strategy – stay focused, and have fun doing it. Most of all remember 'the menu is not the meal'.

Good luck,

Warren

For more information you can:

Call free on 0800 0749289

Visit www.warrenkemp.com

Email info@warrenkemp.com

Write to

Warren Kemp's Recruitment Matters

PO Box 1346 Coventry CV6 3ZF

OTHER PRODUCTS AVAILABLE FROM THE AUTHOR:

"How to Head-Hunt Anyone *you want to*" – a 5 pack cd or tape set with accompanying workbook. (Over 4.5 hours of material)

"25 Ways and More to Grow Your Business" – a generalist marketing book.

"Have I Got A Candidate For You!" – a 12 pack tape set. The audio newsletter for the recruitment industry. (Over 15 hours of material).